MY NAME IS POCAHONTAS

written and illustrated by
WILLIAM ACCORSI

Holiday House / New York

For Vera and Frank Sorensen and family,
and, of course, Eric

Library of Congress Cataloging-in-Publication Data
Accorsi, William.
    My name is Pocahontas / written and illustrated by
William Accorsi.
       p.   cm.
    Summary: The Indian princess describes meeting John Smith
and the other English colonists and eventually traveling
to England to discover more about their culture.
       ISBN 0-8234-0932-5
    1. Pocahontas, d. 1617—Juvenile literature.   2. Powhatan
Indians—Biography—Juvenile literature.   [1. Pocahontas, d. 1617.
2. Powhatan Indians—Biography.   3. Indians of North
America—Biography.]   I. Title.
E99.P85P5714   1992   91–24218   CIP   AC
975.5'01'092—dc20
[B]

Author's Note

My interest in Native Americans began in my boyhood. They have appeared in my sculpture and paintings for the past thirty-five years. I am not an artist who practices ''realism''. I have made use always of that wonderful resource called *artistic license*. Thus the Indians in this book are not rendered as they actually looked in the 1600s. My greater interest is in capturing their spirit.

William Accorsi
June 15, 1991

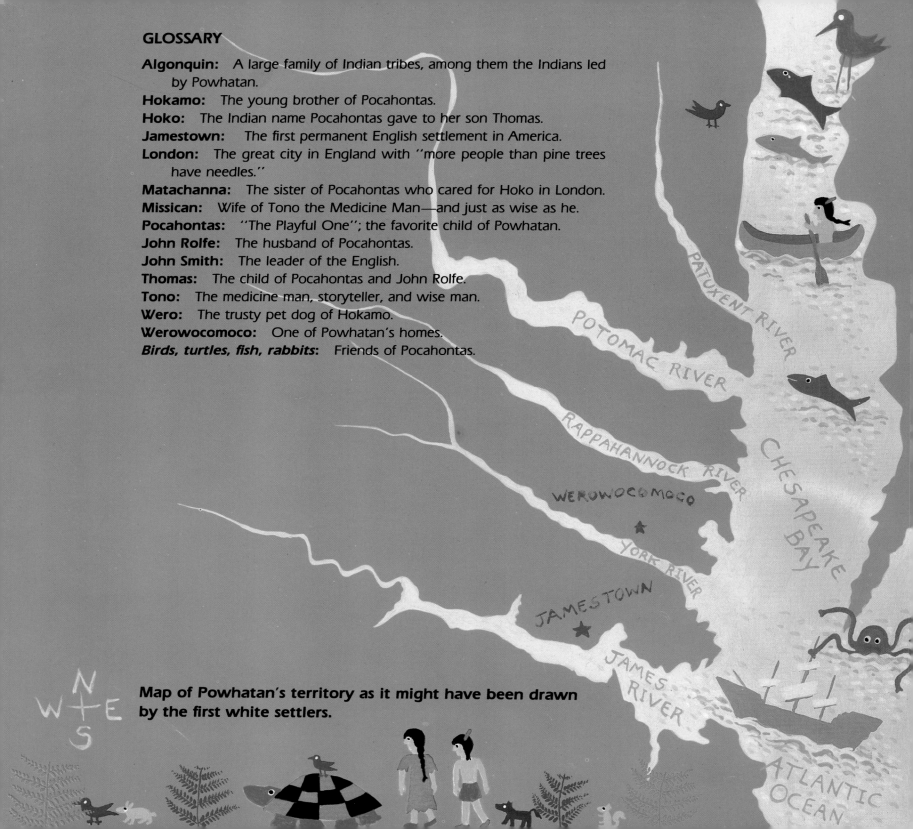

GLOSSARY

Algonquin: A large family of Indian tribes, among them the Indians led by Powhatan.

Hokamo: The young brother of Pocahontas.

Hoko: The Indian name Pocahontas gave to her son Thomas.

Jamestown: The first permanent English settlement in America.

London: The great city in England with "more people than pine trees have needles."

Matachanna: The sister of Pocahontas who cared for Hoko in London.

Missican: Wife of Tono the Medicine Man—and just as wise as he.

Pocahontas: "The Playful One"; the favorite child of Powhatan.

John Rolfe: The husband of Pocahontas.

John Smith: The leader of the English.

Thomas: The child of Pocahontas and John Rolfe.

Tono: The medicine man, storyteller, and wise man.

Wero: The trusty pet dog of Hokamo.

Werowocomoco: One of Powhatan's homes.

Birds, turtles, fish, rabbits: Friends of Pocahontas.

Map of Powhatan's territory as it might have been drawn by the first white settlers.

PATUXENT RIVER

POTOMAC RIVER

RAPPAHANNOCK RIVER

CHESAPEAKE BAY

WEROWOCOMOCO

YORK RIVER

JAMESTOWN

JAMES RIVER

ATLANTIC OCEAN

N W E S

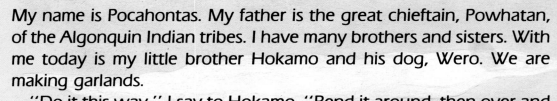

My name is Pocahontas. My father is the great chieftain, Powhatan, of the Algonquin Indian tribes. I have many brothers and sisters. With me today is my little brother Hokamo and his dog, Wero. We are making garlands.

"Do it this way," I say to Hokamo. "Bend it around, then over and under, always carefully, always gently."

"Yes," agrees Hokamo.

Wero says nothing. He watches so he, too, can learn.

"What is the name of this flower?" I ask Hokamo.

"It is called Medicine Man's Toe. The juices are good for mosquito bites."

"Very good! Soon you will know all the plants and animals of the forest."

Finally, the sun is setting. Wero, Hokamo, and I start for the village. We are tired, happy, and very hungry.

Now at home, Hokamo and I take our turtle bowls and sit next to the fire. As we eat, we watch the smoke slowly rise through a hole in the roof. The stars are in the night sky. If we are lucky, Tono, the medicine man, will tell us stories of long ago.

After eating, Hokamo and I go and visit Tono and his wife, Missican.

"Tono, look what we brought you. Flower garlands and plants for your medicine."

"Ah," speaks Tono. "What fine decorations you two have made, and I can use these plants in my medicine. Do you have time for a story?"

"Yes, yes!" Hokamo and I answer.

Tono begins. "One day in the long ago, beyond the highest mountains, lived other tribes of . . ."

Hokamo and I close our eyes and soon are dreaming of the people beyond the highest mountains in the long ago.

Zzzzzzz.

Today is a happy day! Powhatan, our great chieftain and our father, has returned home. He has been visiting other chiefs.

He is with his medicine men and warriors. He looks tired and worried. Hokamo and I wonder what has gone wrong.

Later in the afternoon, I look for Tono the medicine man.

"Tono, why were all the men so serious this morning?"

"The palefaced people have come to our land! They are living down the river where the deep waters begin. These men have hair the color of the sun and hair red like fire."

Men with hair the color of the sun and hair red like fire! I wonder if they are people from the tribe that lives beyond the highest mountains. I want to see them with my own eyes.

I run to the stream to pull my dugout from the sand. My two little shadows are waiting; the one barking, the other talking.

The place where the deep waters begin is less than a day away.
We stay close to shore and pick berries from branches that lean out.
Almost there, we leave the dugout in the tall weeds and walk the
rest of the way.

The sun is high in the sky. The palefaces have built a tall fence of cut trees. We lie outside of the fence in the thick grass. A bird sings—but it is not a bird. It's an Indian signaling that there are other Indians hiding in the tall grass. They, too, are watching the palefaces. The large gate is moving. Someone is coming out.

The first paleface has much yellow-red hair. An Indian in the tall grass jumps up and lets fly an arrow. It glances off the shiny chest of the man. He waves his thunder stick and *Boom!* The Indian brave falls. It is powerful magic! Very frightened, Wero, Hokamo, and I creep quickly through the grass to our canoe.

Now our days are very different. Powhatan has asked Tono to weave a magic spell that will make the palefaces go away. Tono says that his spells no longer work. He speaks again of the tribe beyond the highest mountains.

"I have seen in my dreams peoples of many colors, as numerous as raindrops. One day we shall all live among each other."

My father continues to worry. "When will the palefaces go away?" he wonders.

Some of our people are less worried. The palefaces have shiny beads, tinkling bells, copper kettles, and sharp knives and axes to trade. We have never seen these things before. We gladly exchange corn, fish, and animal skins for these new things.

Confusing days follow. Sometimes we trade with the palefaces. Other times we fight bitterly with them. Their leader is named John Smith. He is from a land called England. One day, my brother and I learn that John Smith has been captured. He is being brought to my father, Powhatan.

Father, the medicine men, and the other chiefs have a meeting to decide what to do with John Smith. I am certain they will do him no harm. Surely they can see he is a strong and brave leader. Yes, they will adopt him into our tribe, then we will learn much about the other peoples.

But no, wait! They intend to kill him! The warriors raise their war clubs. I throw myself to the ground and place my arms around Smith's neck.

"Father! Spare him! Adopt him into our tribe."

It is our custom that one of us may claim a captive, and then that person becomes a member of our tribe. Father looks at me for a long moment. Our people say that of all his many children, I am his favorite.

"From this moment, so be it," says Powhatan. "John Smith, now you are the brother of Pocahontas, and I am father to you both."

Hokamo, Wero, and I spend hours each day with John Smith. He tells us of the great village across the sea called London, where there are more English people than pine trees have needles. I tell John Smith of the medicine man's dream of the many different kinds of people beyond the highest mountains.

"Yes," says Smith. "The world is larger than we yet know. There are far more tribes than we could ever count."

After many days, John Smith tells Father he wants to visit his own people. Father doesn't want him to go, but Smith answers he will send wonderful gifts in return. Father asks for a large magic boom-stick called a cannon. Smith says he will try to get one, and Father sends some men along to bring it back. When they reach Jamestown, Smith shows the braves the cannon. They try and try but cannot move it. It weighs as much as a small mountain. The men return instead with many smaller gifts.

John Smith has now been away for several days. We miss him and his colorful stories of the other peoples and the different lands over the great ocean. With Hokamo, Wero, and some of my young friends, I travel to visit Smith at the place they call Jamestown. There I am able to learn more of the English language, and John Smith is able to learn more of mine.

Hokamo, Wero, and I return home. After several weeks, we hear that John Smith has disappeared. This is not unusual because Smith often leaves Jamestown to explore and trade with other tribes. We ask again and again, "Where is John Smith?"

Finally the English answer, "He is dead. He has been dead for some time."

Dead? How could John Smith be dead? He was so young, strong, and full of life. I am very sad. My new brother and teacher—gone! But Powhatan is happy with the news. With John Smith dead, Father sees his chance to get rid of all the palefaces. He sends warriors to destroy them.

The fighting continues for months between our people and the English. The great sailing ships bring more palefaces to our land. I remember what John Smith once said, "There are more English people than pine trees have needles." If Smith were alive, he could stop the fighting. Now, there is no one to make peace.

I'm growing older and becoming a young woman. My carefree days are passing by.

Suddenly I am placed in the middle of the conflict between my people and the English. The palefaces trick me to go aboard an English ship in the river. The captain and his men sail to Jamestown, with me as their prisoner.

The English treat me well at Jamestown. They dress me in the clothing of a palefaced woman. They send word to my father that they'll give me back if he will trade corn and return the weapons he has captured from them in battle.

Father sends some corn and a few broken weapons. He will not give in to all their demands.

Each day the English teach me more of their language and religion. Weeks go by and months pass. Father doesn't come for me, and I don't know what to do.

There is an Englishman, John Rolfe, who visits me daily. He wishes to marry me. I like him and cannot decide what to do. Some of my family come to Jamestown to see if I am being well treated. Hokamo says that he doesn't think Powhatan will ever give in to the demands of the English

"If that is so, tell Father I will stay with the English. I will marry John Rolfe. Then perhaps Father will stop fighting."

John Rolfe again asks to marry me. I answer John, "If our marriage will bring peace between your people and mine, then I will happily marry you."

With the news of our coming wedding, the fighting between our peoples comes to an end.

The following year is very peaceful. To everyone's delight, I give birth to a baby boy. John Rolfe gives our son the English name, Thomas. But I call him Hoko to remind me of my younger brother, Hokamo. John wants me to visit London, England. I will be happy to see the many new tribes of people, but sad to leave my Indian friends. My sister Matachanna and ten of our tribe will come with us.

Hokamo, Wero, and our friends wave from shore as we set sail.

London, England, is larger than all of Powhatan's forests. I am taken to meet the English king and queen. They introduce me as "Pocahontas, Indian Princess, Daughter of the Great Powhatan." I am proud of myself and my people.

Then, to my great surprise, I learn that John Smith is alive and living in London.

Days pass. One morning I am told a visitor is at the door. It is John Smith. Alive! I am surprised and happy to see him, but I am also angry. I say, "My father spared your life and made you my brother. Why did you leave our land and let people think you no longer lived? And why have you waited so long to visit me in London?"

John Smith explains that he had become ill and returned to England to get well. We talk on and on and once again become as brother and sister.

My husband, John Rolfe, has told me that an artist will paint a picture of me. This makes me happy because people who have not seen me will be able to tell what I look like. The artist comes each day to work on my portrait, and almost every day there are visitors to meet me. They seem surprised that I speak their language so well.

They say to each other, "Can you believe it? Look at her, an Indian princess."

Again, I am proud of myself and my people. I look at my dear son, little Hoko. Someday he will return to the land of Powhatan. It is my hope there will be peace among all peoples by then.

Pocahontas never returned to her native land. She died in London shortly after John Smith's visit. Her son Thomas (Hoko) grew up in England and later went to America. Today, Pocahontas, the "first lady" of Native Americans, is remembered for her kindness and love for all people.